Șerban Eugen Savu

SHORT HISTORY OF THE MASONIC RITUALS

Lux Mundi

2024

Descrierea CIP a Bibliotecii Naţionale a României

SAVU, ŞERBAN EUGEN

Short history of the masonic rituals / Şerban Eugen Savu. - Bucureşti : Lux Mundi, 2024

ISBN 978-630-6652-09-9

061.236.6

Book design & cover: Oana Savu

editura@luxmundi.ro

EARLY YEARS

The origins and development of Masonic rituals are deeply intertwined with the rise of speculative Freemasonry in early 18th-century England.

During this formative period, which extended until 1738, the pivotal three degrees laid the foundation of symbolic Freemasonry. This era began a rich tradition of rituals that defined the Masonic experience.

By 1751, a significant reorganization occurred within English Freemasonry, establishing two predominant factions: the "Moderns" and the "Ancients."

Two distinct Grand Lodges represented these factions, embodying different currents of Masonic thought and practice.

This division highlighted Masonic principles' diverse interpretations and applications and set the stage for Freemasonry's future expansion and evolution.

As Freemasonry spread beyond the borders of England, it embraced new dimensions, most notably through the introduction of the "High Degrees," particularly those associated with the Scottish and

York rites.

This period, stretching from the mid-17th century to the dawn of the 19th century, witnessed the birth and refinement of most Masonic rituals associated with the symbolic degrees and those related to the degrees of various perfection rites.

This expansive phase in Masonic history was characterized by a rich tapestry of rituals that reflected the evolving Masonic ideology and a testament to the enduring appeal of its mysteries.

The creation and development of these rituals underscored the dynamic nature of Freemasonry, adapting to new cultures and contexts while preserving the core elements of its ancient heritage.

The rituals associated with the symbolic degrees, which emerged during that significant period, continue to be practiced in contemporary Freemasonry, albeit with minor adjustments.

These modifications reflect the unique characteristics of each Grand Lodge, including cultural

nuances, linguistic translations, and other specific elements. Despite these changes, the rituals retain their foundational essence, preserving the original spirit and purpose central to their practice since inception.

The nuances of the rituals for each degree and the specificities of various Masonic ceremonies are shaped by the broader framework they are part of, whether it be a rite or a complete Masonic system.

This framework varies by region and tradition. It is known as *"Rite"* in the French context, *"Complete Masonic System"* in American English, and *"Working"* within the British Masonic vernacular.

These terminologies reflect the diverse approaches and interpretations within the global Masonic community, each contributing to the rich tapestry of Masonic ritual practice.

This diversity allows for a vibrant exchange of ideas and practices within Freemasonry, ensuring that while the core principles remain unchanged, the expression of these principles can adapt and evolve.

This adaptability ensures that Masonic rituals remain relevant and resonant with members across different cultures and epochs, linking them to a shared heritage while embracing the uniqueness of their local contexts.

Grand Lodges oversee the foundational first three degrees in every Rite or Complete Masonic System.

These initial degrees form the bedrock of Freemasonry, guiding members through the initial

stages of their Masonic journey. Beyond these, the higher degrees are governed by distinct Masonic bodies, each with its structure and area of focus.

This separation ensures specialized stewardship over Freemasonry's diverse aspects and teachings, allowing for a deeper exploration of its principles and mysteries.

An exception to this structure is found in England, where the "*Mark Mason and Holly Royal Arch*" degrees, considered by many to be the completion of the third degree, are directly administered by the United Grand Lodge of England.

This arrangement underscores the unique position of the Mark Mason and Holly Royal Arch within English Freemasonry, integrating it more closely with the foundational degrees and highlighting its significance within the broader Masonic tradition.

This dual governance system reflects Freemasonry's layered and multifaceted nature, with the Grand Lodges providing a unified foundation for the Masonic

journey. At the same time, the independent Masonic entities offer pathways to further enlightenment and understanding.

Trough this structure, Freemasonry fosters a comprehensive and cohesive experience for its members, nurturing their personal and spiritual growth across various degrees and disciplines.

RITUAL DIFFERENCES

Understanding the diversity within Freemasonry's rituals requires acknowledging its global spread, which began well before 1731 when the English Masonic ritual was still taking shape.

The transmission of Masonic practices worldwide

didn't come from a singular, unified source but from multiple origins, not in a complete form. This fragmented dissemination contributed to the rich tapestry of rituals observed today.

The division within England's first Grand Lodge in 1753, which led to the emergence of two distinct Grand Lodges - the "Ancients" (a newer, breakaway group) and the "Moderns" (the older, original Grand Lodge) - further complicated the landscape.

Each faction developed its version of the Masonic

ritual, imbuing the practices with their unique interpretations and emphases.

Consequently, the rituals we observe today are not uniform; they often draw upon the traditions of both the Ancients and the Moderns and, in many cases, blend elements of both.

This historical backdrop highlights the evolutionary nature of the Masonic ritual and explains the variance found in Masonic practices around the globe. It underscores Freemasonry's adaptability, which can incorporate various influences while maintaining a cohesive identity. It illustrates the fraternity's resilience and flexibility in the face of internal divisions and external changes.

The practice of literal ritualism, emphasizing precise wording and uniformity, is a relatively recent development within Freemasonry's long history.

Initially, the "mouth-to-ear" method of transmitting Masonic knowledge was less about rote memorizing specific words and more about imparting essential information and principles. This approach allowed for a certain fluidity and adaptability in how Masonic teachings were shared among members.

As Freemasonry expanded and Grand Lodges were established, they often came into being through the unification of various individual Lodges.

Each of these Lodges might have been practicing a version of Masonic ritual derived from a different source.

Consequently, the rituals eventually adopted by these Grand Lodges often represented a synthesis of multiple traditions. This amalgamation process resulted in the rich and diverse ritual practices observed within Freemasonry today.

This historical evolution reflects Freemasonry's capacity to integrate a variety of influences and practices, ensuring that its rituals remain a living tradition that can adapt to the needs and circumstances of its members. It underscores the fraternity's commitment to the core principles of Masonic teaching, even as it embraces the variety and diversity that come from its broad geographical spread and the unique heritage of its constituent Lodges.

Within Freemasonry, certain core elements and structures are universally observed across all Lodges regardless of the jurisdiction or specific ritual practiced.

These fundamental components include the presence of a Master and two Wardens, who are integral to the Lodge's governance and ceremonial proceedings.

Additionally, each Lodge appoints a Secretary and Treasurer to manage its administrative and financial affairs.

At the heart of every Lodge is the Altar, upon which are placed the three Great Lights of Freemasonry: The Holy Book (representing spiritual guidance), the Square (symbolizing morality), and the Compass (denoting the boundaries of personal conduct).

Other significant symbols, called the Great Lights, play crucial roles in Masonic rituals and teaching.

The structure of Freemasonry is built around three degrees, each designed to impart specific lessons and moral philosophies to its members.

Admission to the fraternity is highly selective, requiring a unanimous ballot to ensure that only worthy candidates are made Masons and membership is exclusively male.

A Substitute Word is consistently imparted to the candidate during initiation, serving as a symbolic key to Masonic teachings.

Furthermore, every Lodge is securely tiled, which means it is protected from the intrusion of non-members, ensuring the privacy and sanctity of its proceedings.

Rituals for opening and closing the Lodge are performed with ceremonial precision, marking the beginning and end of Masonic activities.

These rituals, steeped in tradition and symbolism, reinforce the fraternity's values and unity.

Universal elements underscore the shared identity

and principles that bind Freemasons worldwide despite the diversity of their individual practices and cultural backgrounds.

They represent the foundational pillars upon which the global fraternity of Freemasonry stands, fostering a sense of brotherhood and continuity across the ages.

All Masonic rituals, in varying degrees, incorporate drama and exemplification elements, particularly within the Master's Degree.

The extent and manner of these dramatizations can differ significantly from one jurisdiction to another, reflecting the rich diversity of Masonic tradition. These dramatic elements are not merely for the ceremony but serve to deepen the symbolic and educational impact of the rituals.

Despite these and a few other foundational practices, the Masonic ritual has various variations.

For instance, how aprons are worn during ceremonies illustrates this diversity; an apron may be positioned differently in the same degree, depending on the jurisdiction.

This variation in practice underscores Freemasonry's adaptability and cultural specificity, allowing it to resonate with members across different geographical and cultural landscapes while maintaining its core principles and teachings.

The organizational structure and ceremonial practices of Masonic Lodges can vary significantly across different jurisdictions.

For instance, the number of officers present within a Lodge may differ, reflecting each jurisdiction's specific traditions and administrative needs.

The procedure for opening and closing Lodges also illustrates this diversity. While some jurisdictions traditionally open and close their meetings on the Master Mason's Degree, others may do so on the First Degree or choose to open and close in the degree relevant to the day's work.

In certain jurisdictions, such as England, the

role of the Immediate Past Master (I∴P∴M∴) is of considerable importance, as it plays a significant part in Lodge activities.

Conversely, this position may not be recognized or utilized in other Lodges that practice Rituals different in origin from that of England's Jurisdiction (Emulation Rituals).

Additionally, the presence of specific roles within the Lodge, such as Inner Guards or Masters of Ceremonies, can vary.

Some Lodges may incorporate these positions into their standard officer lineup, while others may not.

Even the practices of dividing, lettering, and syllabling (the methods used to teach and convey Masonic knowledge) demonstrate a wide range of approaches, almost as diverse as the number of Masonic Jurisdictions themselves.

These variations highlight the rich tapestry of Masonic tradition, showing how Freemasonry adapts and evolves to fit its members' cultural and organizational contexts worldwide while maintaining the foundational principles that unite Freemasons worldwide.

KEY SOURCES OF RITUALS

To better understand the origins and diversity of Masonic rituals, it's helpful to consider the key sources Freemasonry has drawn over the years.

These primary influences include:

The Mother Grand Lodge of England (1717-1753)

The foundational body of modern Freemasonry, established in 1717, set the precedent for Masonic practices and organization.

The Grand Lodge of the "Ancients" (1753-1813)

A faction emerged in response to perceived innovations by the original Grand Lodge, advocating a return to older practices.

The Grand Lodge of the "Moderns" (1753-1813)

The original Grand Lodge, which continued to

evolve during this period, was often seen as adopting a more progressive approach to the Masonic ritual.

The United Grand Lodge (1813 and on)

It was formed from the union of the "Ancients" and the "Moderns," marking the beginning of a unified Masonic practice in England.

The Grand Lodge of Ireland (1724 and on)

An independent body that has contributed significantly to the spread and development of

Freemasonry with its unique traditions.

The Grand Lodge of Scotland (1736 and on)

Another independent Masonic body is known for its distinctive rituals and significant influence on global Freemasonry.

Pre-Grand Lodge era Lodges of England, Ireland, and Scotland

Various older lodges existed before the formal

establishment of Grand Lodges contributed ancient practices and traditions to the mosaic of Freemasonry.

These sources collectively represent Freemasonry's rich and varied heritage, highlighting the evolution and adaptation of its rituals and practices through centuries.

Each has shaped the Masonic world, contributing unique elements woven into the fabric of the fraternity's global tapestry.

For historians, the diversity of Masonic origins does not represent a straightforward narrative of six or seven distinct and "pure" sources of ritual. Instead, the evolution of these rituals is marked by complexity and continuous transformation.

The practices set forth by the original Grand Lodge, established in 1717, underwent significant changes over the years, reflecting the dynamic nature of Masonic tradition.

The emergence of the Grand Lodges of the "Ancients" and the "Moderns" introduced further alterations to the Masonic ritual, each body adjusting to the established rites.

These modifications were substantial enough that members of one faction often found it challenging to be recognized Masonically by the other, highlighting the degree of divergence between these two branches of Freemasonry.

This evolving landscape underscores the fluidity of Masonic practice and its challenges for those seeking to trace its historical development.

Rather than a set of unaltered traditions passed down through generations, the Masonic ritual is characterized by its adaptability and the influence of various Masonic bodies over time, each contributing to the rich tapestry of the fraternity's global heritage.

The ritual practiced by the Mother Grand Lodge from 1717 to 1753 underwent significant evolution by the time the United Grand Lodge was established in 1813, following the reconciliation of the two factions originally part of the Mother Grand Lodge - the "Ancients" and the "Moderns."

This reconciliation marked a pivotal moment in Masonic history, leading to the creation of a unified body known as the United Grand Lodge, or the Grand Lodge of Reconciliation.

In forming its ritual, the United Grand Lodge undertook a selective synthesis process, drawing from the best elements of the divergent practices of the "Ancients" and the "Moderns."

This approach aimed to harmonize the differences that had previously divided the fraternity, creating a cohesive ritual framework that could unite Masons under a standard banner. This new ritual was not simply a return to the original Mother Grand Lodge practices. Still, it represented a refined amalgamation of Masonic traditions, reflecting a commitment to unity and the shared principles of Freemasonry.

As Freemasonry upholds and honors the core Landmarks universally acknowledged across its diverse spectrum - principles eloquently summarized by Joseph Fort Newton as "The fatherhood of God, the Brotherhood of Man, the Moral Law, the Golden Rule, and the hope of Life Everlasting" - the significance of variations in ritual expression and teaching methods diminishes.

These variations reflect the fraternity's rich tapestry of cultural and historical contexts.

Freemasons across different eras and regions have discovered multiple ways to articulate and impart the timeless truths of this venerable craft.

This diversity in approach underscores the adaptability of Freemasonry, demonstrating its capacity to resonate with members from varied backgrounds while steadfastly maintaining its foundational principles.

THE MOST PRACTICED RITUALS IN THE WORLD

Today, the landscape of Freemasonry is marked by the diversity of its rituals, each with its own unique heritage and set of practices.

Among the most widely practiced rituals across the globe are:

The "Emulation" Ritual

Originating in England, this ritual is celebrated for its structured precision and depth, embodying the essence of traditional Masonic practice.

U.S. Rituals

It is a collective term for the various rituals practiced within the United States, each reflecting the rich mosaic of American Masonic history and culture.

The Ritual of the Symbolic Degrees of the Ancient and Accepted Scottish Rite

Known for its comprehensive system of degrees, this ritual offers a nuanced exploration of Masonic symbolism and philosophy.

The Ritual of the Symbolic Degrees of the French Rite

Reflecting France's unique contribution to Freemasonry, this rite integrates French culture and philosophical thought elements into the Masonic tradition.

The Ritual of the Symbolic Degrees of the Ancient and Primitive Rite of Memphis-Mizraim

After 1881, these Rites began to regroup Masons of the Grand Orient of France and of the Ancient and Accepted Scottish Rite who were interested in the studies of the esoterics of Masonic symbolism: Gnosis, Kabbalah, even Hermetics and Occultism.

The Ritual of the Symbolic Degrees of the Swedish Rite

Distinctive for its Christian orientation, this rite is a testament to the adaptability of Masonic practice to local religious and cultural contexts.

The Ritual of the Symbolic Degrees of the Rectified Scottish Rite

This rite emphasizes spiritual and moral refinement, offering a path that is both contemplative and rigorous.

The Schroeder Ritual

Praised for its simplicity and clarity, this German ritual focuses on Freemasonry's core ethical teachings, making it accessible and resonant.

These rituals represent Freemasonry's rich and varied tapestry, each contributing to the global fraternity's goals of moral improvement, fraternal bonds, and philosophical inquiry.

Despite their differences, these rituals share common

themes of enlightenment, virtue, and brotherly love, reflecting the universal principles at the heart of Freemasonry.

THE RITUALS OF THE TWO GRAND LODGES OF ENGLAND

(BEFORE 1813)

In 1716, a pivotal moment in Freemasonry occurred when four Lodges in London came together to establish the foundation of the first Grand Lodge.

This seminal event marked a new chapter in the Masonic tradition, culminating in its inaugural assembly on June 24, 1717.

It was a significant step towards formalizing the structure and governance of Freemasonry, setting a precedent for the organization and unity of Lodges under a central authority.

During the decade that followed, specifically between 1720 and 1730, the Grand Lodge of London began to shape its first ritual. This period was crucial for developing and formalizing the practices defining the Masonic experience.

However, in 1730, a pivotal incident occurred that would challenge the secrecy and sanctity of Masonic rites.

Samuel Prichard's publication, "Masonry Dissected," exposed the ritual to the public, revealing the Sacred

Words and Passwords integral to Masonic meetings. This unauthorized disclosure forced the Grand Lodge to take immediate action to protect the integrity of their gatherings.

In response, the Grand Lodge implemented changes to the Sacred Words and Passwords, a necessary measure to preserve the exclusivity and privacy of Freemasonry.

This move aimed to prevent uninitiated individuals from infiltrating Masonic meetings in London,

ensuring that only bona fide members could participate in the rituals and discussions within the Lodge.

This incident underscores the importance of secrecy and trust within Freemasonry, highlighting the challenges of maintaining the confidentiality of its practices in the face of external breaches.

The Grand Lodge reaffirmed its commitment to Freemasonry's core principles through adaptation and resilience, securing its traditions for future generations.

Establishing the first Grand Lodge was a watershed

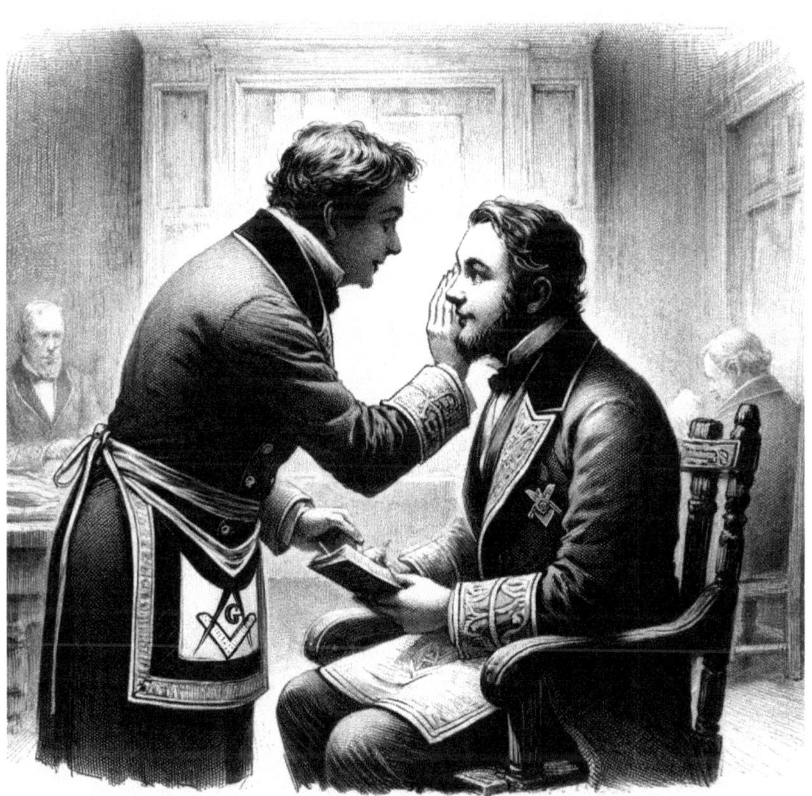

moment in Freemasonry's history. It introduced several innovative practices that significantly modernized and transformed the Order.

This period of change has sparked various reactions among Masons, particularly concerning the inclusivity of the Lodges operating under the Grand Lodge's jurisdiction.

These Lodges adopted a policy of exclusivity, preferring initiates who were men from the aristocracy. This stance effectively barred regular Irish Masons, whether residents or visitors in London, from joining their ranks.

The exclusion of Irish Masons and the introduction of specific innovations in the ritual practices of the first Grand Lodge led to growing discontent among some members who were deeply attached to Freemasonry's traditional values.

In response to these developments, a faction within the community, yearning to preserve Freemasonry's original ethos and practices, decided to dissociate from the first Grand Lodge.

Their allegiance shifted towards the principles upheld by the Irish Grand Lodge, reflecting a desire to maintain a more inclusive and traditional approach to Masonic rituals.

This schism was instrumental in forming the Grand Lodge of the Ancients in 1751, marking a significant moment in Masonic history.

The Grand Lodge of the Ancients positioned itself

as a bastion of traditional Masonic values, offering an alternative to those who felt alienated by the first Grand Lodge's modernizing reforms.

This division within the Masonic community highlighted the tension between innovation and tradition. This theme has recurred throughout Freemasonry's history, shaping its development and the diversity of practices observed within the Order today.

The formation of what came to be known as the

Grand Lodge of the Ancients was officially titled "*The Grand Committee of the Oldest and most Honorable Fraternity of Free and Accepted Masons, according to the old Institutions.*"

This title reflected their commitment to adhering to Freemasonry's foundational principles and practices.

Ironically, these members referred to the earlier established Grand Lodge of London as "*The Grand Lodge of Moderns,*" highlighting their view of the latter's departure from traditional Masonic values and

practices.

The Grand Lodge of the Ancients, drawing heavily from a demographic rich in Irish emigrants, embarked on developing a new ritual.

This ritual was deeply influenced by practices prevalent in Ireland and Scotland, aiming to realign more closely with the traditions of operative masonry that were common before the establishment of the first Grand Lodge in 1717.

Their efforts culminated in the publication of "*Three*

Distinct Knocks" in 1760, a seminal work that offered a comprehensive outline of their ritual practices.

This new ritual was not merely a return to older practices. Still, it represented a deliberate effort to preserve a version of Freemasonry that the Ancients believed was more authentic to its roots.

By incorporating elements closer to the operative masonry traditions, the Grand Lodge of the Ancients sought to distinguish themselves from the innovations introduced by the Grand Lodge of Moderns, advocating

for a continuity that they felt had been disrupted.

The contrasting approaches between the Ancients and the Moderns underscored a broader debate within Freemasonry about the balance between tradition and innovation. This theme continues to resonate within the Masonic world.

The establishment of the Grand Lodge of the Ancients and their adoption of a ritual steeped in the practices of Irish and Scottish Freemasonry contributed significantly to the diversity of Masonic expression and the ongoing dialogue about the essence and direction of Freemasonry.

THE RITUAL OF THE UNITED GRAND LODGE OF ENGLAND

(AFTER 1813)

In 1752, a significant event occurred within the Grand Lodge of the Ancients when Laurence Dermott was elected as Grand Secretary.

His election marked the beginning of a pivotal era for the Ancients. Dermott's contributions were profound, notably through his "Ahiman Rezon" authorship in 1756.

This document, which came to serve as the Constitution of the Grand Lodge of the Ancients, played a crucial role in defining the identity and principles of this faction within Freemasonry. Dermott's assertion within the document that the "*Royal Arch is the root, the heart and the marrow of Freemasonry*" underscored his and his contemporaries' importance on this degree,

setting it apart from the more limited scope recognized by their counterparts, the Moderns.

The distinction between the Ancients and the Moderns was stark in their recognition and practice of Masonic degrees.

While the Moderns confined their recognition to the initial symbolic degrees, the Ancients embraced the "Royal Arch" as a fundamental component of Masonic practice, indicative of its roots in operative masonry.

This degree, along with the "Mark Master Mason"

degree, was readily practiced within lodges under the Ancients' jurisdiction without special permission. This open practice attracted even members of the Moderns, who, despite official prohibitions, were drawn to the "Royal Arch" and its rich symbolic significance.

This crossover of adherence to the "Royal Arch" degree by members of the Moderns highlighted a growing appreciation for the depth it added to the Masonic journey despite initial resistance.

Eventually, this led to a significant shift within the

Grand Lodge of London, which came to recognize and formally admit the "Royal Arch" as an integral extension of the third degree rather than merely a supplementary addition.

This acknowledgment represented a convergence of views between the Ancients and Moderns, illustrating the dynamic nature of Freemasonry and its ability to evolve and incorporate diverse perspectives within its practices.

The "Royal Arch" as a complementary part of the third degree by the Grand Lodge of London marked a reconciliation, bridging a divide that had previously distinguished the Ancients from the Moderns in their approach to Masonic degrees.

In the landscape of English Freemasonry, a pivotal figure emerged in the form of William Preston, whose efforts marked a significant attempt to bridge the ritualistic divide between the "Ancients" and "Moderns."

In a time when Masonic teachings and communications were predominantly oral, Preston embarked on a meticulous project to compile the catechisms and instructions associated with various degrees.

His endeavor led to the creation of what would be known as the written rituals, a groundbreaking development in the preservation and standardization of Masonic practice.

The result of Preston's efforts, famously known as the *"Prestonian Lectures,"* not only served as a vital

repository of Masonic knowledge and laid the foundational framework for the "York" type rituals.

These rituals, developed and interpreted from Preston's lectures, drew inspiration from his comprehensive approach to Masonic education and ritual organization. His seminal work, *"Illustrations of Masonry,"* first published in 1772, became a cornerstone text.

The significance of Preston's contributions was reflected in the repeated reprinting of his work after 1775, underscoring its widespread influence and utility in English Masonic circles up until 1813.

Preston's legacy in Freemasonry is characterized by his innovative approach to consolidating and codifying Masonic rituals and teachings.

By transitioning these practices from oral tradition to written documentation, he facilitated a more unified understanding of Masonic rituals and ensured their preservation for future generations. His work paved the way for a more integrated approach to Freemasonry in England, contributing to the eventual reconciliation and unification of the "*Ancients*" and "*Moderns*." The "*Prestonian Lectures*" and "*Illustrations of Masonry*" remain enduring testaments to Preston's vision and dedication to the craft, embodying a pivotal moment in the evolution of Masonic practice.

In a significant turning point for English Freemasonry, 1813 marked the unification of the two Grand Lodges, a process that required the creation of new, consolidated rituals. Dr. Samuel Hemming was entrusted with this critical task, a responsibility he undertook with the assistance of William Williams.

Their work involved carefully revising William Preston's earlier texts, during which they decided to eliminate certain elements to craft rituals that would be more universally acceptable within the Masonic community.

Notably, Hemming removed references to the New Testament, a move aimed at honoring Freemasonry's principle of universality, ensuring that members of all religious backgrounds could embrace its teachings and rituals.

Following this significant endeavor, Hemming founded the *"Emulation Lodge of Improvement"* in 1823, an initiative to promote the practice and perfection of these newly formulated rituals.

It was here that the "Emulation" ritual was published for the first time, offering a standardized approach to Masonic practice that was rooted in the principles of unity and inclusivity established during the unification process.

Despite these efforts to unify Masonic rituals under

the "Emulation" framework, the landscape of English Freemasonry remained diverse in its ritualistic practices.

Even today, several different rituals are practiced within England, reflecting the rich tapestry of Masonic tradition and the individual Lodges' preferences for certain ritualistic elements over others.

This diversity underscores the dynamic nature of Freemasonry, a space where unity and variation coexist. Members can explore the depth and breadth

of Masonic teachings in a manner that resonates with their understanding and experience of the craft.

The process initiated by Hemming and Williams and the subsequent establishment of the *"Emulation Lodge of Improvement"* represent pivotal moments in the ongoing evolution of Masonic ritual practice.

These developments highlight the balance Freemasonry seeks between preserving its core values and principles while accommodating its global membership's diverse perspectives and traditions.

THE RITUALS PRACTICED IN THE UNITED STATES

As speculative Freemasonry was taking shape in England, the seeds of the fraternity were also being sown across the Atlantic in the American colonies.

This expansion was primarily driven by the presence of colonial troops and the deployment of military garrisons in these strategically significant yet tumultuous regions.

The earliest documented evidence of a Masonic Lodge holding meetings in what would become the United States dates back to before 1730, indicating the early establishment and practice of Freemasonry on American soil.

Between 1731 and 1775, the period saw a spirited competition among the English Grand Lodges and the Grand Lodges of Ireland and Scotland.

Each was keen to extend its influence and establish new Lodges under its jurisdiction in the burgeoning colonies.

This expansion era laid the groundwork for Freemasonry's role in American society, mainly as the colonies edged closer to the pivotal struggle for independence.

By the outbreak of the American Revolutionary War in 1775, there were already over 100 Lodges operating under English auspices, a testament to the fraternity's rapid growth and appeal.

Interestingly, the tumult and division of the war years from 1775 to 1783 did not hinder the establishment of new Lodges.

On the contrary, Freemasonry continued to flourish, with new Lodges emerging to serve members on both sides of the conflict. This growth during a period of profound upheaval and division highlights the unifying appeal of Freemasonry, offering a sense of fraternity and stability amidst the uncertainties of war.

The spread of Freemasonry in the American colonies and its continued expansion during the Revolutionary War underscores the fraternity's adaptability and the universal appeal of its principles.

Freemasonry provided a common ground for men of varied backgrounds and beliefs, fostering a sense of brotherhood and mutual support that transcended the polarities of wartime allegiances.

Over time, the Masonic Lodges established in the U.S. began to incorporate the "*Mark Master Mason*" and "*Royal Arch*" degrees practiced in England, albeit with variations in rituals and Constitutions from one Lodge to another.

The diversity in practice highlighted the need for a more unified approach to Freemasonry across the burgeoning nation. Enter Thomas Smith Webb, a figure pivotal in the quest for harmonizing American

Freemasonry. Drawing upon the foundational work of William Preston, Webb sought to adapt and apply these principles within the American context.

His efforts culminated in publishing "Freemasons' Monitor and Illustrations of Freemasonry" in 1797, with a subsequent reprint in 1802.

This work, through its various editions expanding until 1869, gradually incorporated rituals of the "Chapter," "Cryptic," and "Chivalric" degrees associated with the York Rite, aiming to offer a comprehensive guide to the Masonic journey.

While Webb aspired to establish a *"Uniform Standard Work"* that could be adopted by all American Lodges, the outcome was somewhat different.

Today, each Grand Lodge in the United States operates under its version of the Masonic ritual.

However, the variations among these rituals are relatively minor, and some scholars have collectively referred to them as *"The American Rite."*

This term suggests uniformity in Freemasonry's core principles and practices across the United States, even if specific details and rituals vary from jurisdiction to jurisdiction.

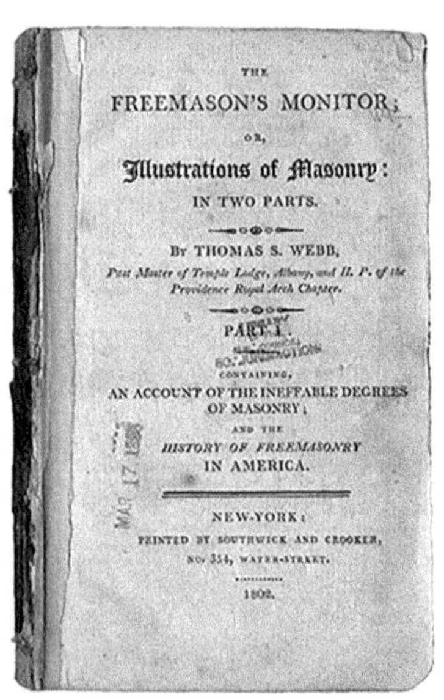

Webb's legacy, therefore, lies not in creating a universally adopted standard work but in his significant influence on shaping American Freemasonry.

By adapting and promoting a work system that drew heavily from Preston's teachings and the rich York Rite traditions, Webb helped forge a distinctly American interpretation of Freemasonry that balanced uniformity with the flexibility to accommodate local traditions and preferences.

This balance has allowed Freemasonry to thrive in the diverse and dynamic landscape of the United States, maintaining a cohesive identity while respecting the individual character of each Grand Lodge.

THE RITUAL OF THE SYMBOLIC DEGREES OF THE ANCIENT AND ACCEPTED SCOTTISH RITE

The narrative of this particular ritual is deeply entwined with the evolution of the *"High Scottish Degrees"* in France, a development sparked by a seminal event: the address delivered by Knight Andrew Michael Ramsay on March 21, 1737, at a Masonic gathering in Paris, the specific Lodge of which remains unnamed.

Ramsay's speech, emphasizing Freemasonry's chivalric and historical dimensions, catalyzed the formation of what would become known as the High Degrees, enriching the Masonic landscape with a new depth of ritual and symbolism.

His speech became important for Freemasonry because it was the basis of the conflict with the

Vatican, which became official in 1738 when Pope Clement XII condemned Freemasonry.

In 1737, Ramsay was the Grand Orator of a Masonic body/order in Paris and wrote the "*Discourse delivered at the initiation of the Freemasons.*" Indeed, his membership of the "*Knights of St Lazarus of Jerusalem*" could have inspired him in his work, which he felt should be considered by the dominant religious authority of the time.

Thus, he sent the text to Cardinal Fleury, asking the

Church's blessing on the principles of Freemasonry as he had expressed them: *"The obligations imposed by the order are to protect your brethren by your authority, to enlighten them by your knowledge, to illuminate them by your virtues, to help them in their necessities, to sacrifice all personal resentments, and to strive after all that may contribute to the peace and unity of society."*

Confusion is always made when Ramsay mentions the Knights Templar in his speech when he mentions the Knights Hospitaller. Those aware of the issues of that period understood his mention of the Crusader Knights to be an indirect reference to the Knights Templar.

For a Catholic Church expanding the Society of Jesus (Jesuit Order) at that time, the concept of Masonic ritual or any connection with the Knights Templar was utterly inappropriate, even absurd.

To Ramsay's letter of March 20, 1737, Cardinal Fleury's reply came quickly, by the end of that March. The Cardinal decided to ban all Masonic meetings.

Cardinal André-Hercule de Fleury was the first minister of Louis XV of France. Due to the political conjunctures of the

time and the struggles between sympathizers of the Royal Houses of Stuart and James, sympathizers from the ranks of whom some had been initiated into Masonic Lodges, to avoid any risk, Fleury urged Pope Clement XII to issue a bull forbidding all Roman Catholics to become Freemasons under threat of excommunication.

Thus, in the year immediately following Ramsay's initiative, on 28 April 1738, Pope Clement XII first condemned Freemasonry by issuing the Papal Bull "*In eminenti apostolatus specula*," in which he forbade Catholics to become Freemasons.

Returning to Chevalier Ramsay and his "*Discourse pronounced at the reception of Freemasons by Monsieur de Ramsay,*" he was the first to present a firm public position (in a Masonic setting) that changed the perception of the origin of Freemasonry.

"Our founders were not mere stonecutters, nor were they curious geniuses who delved into research. They were not just skilled architects hired to build material temples. They were also religious leaders and experienced warriors who understood the wisdom of engaging in spiritual temple building. King Solomon wrote our statutes, maxims, and mysteries in hieroglyphic characters, which were put into the original code of our order.

After the destruction of the first Temple, Zerubbabel - the Grand Master of the Jerusalem Lodge - was commissioned by Cyrus the Great to lay the foundation

of the second Great Temple in Jerusalem, where he deposited the mysterious Book of Solomon.

This book was lost until the Crusades when part of it was found after the liberation of Jerusalem.

Kings, princes, and knights returned from the Crusades to their countries and founded various Masonic Lodges there."

In response to these degrees' burgeoning interest and complexity, Masonic brethren in France they organized themselves into various Chapters and Councils to oversee and administer the rites.

Among these was the "Sovereign Council of the East and West Emperors," which took a pivotal role in codifying a structured system of degrees.

This body developed a comprehensive 25-degree Rite known as the *"Rite of Perfection."* This Rite laid the foundational elements for what would eventually evolve into the Ancient and Accepted Scottish Rite, marking a significant milestone in the history of Freemasonry.

Brother Stephen (Étienne) Morin emerged as a key figure in this period of Masonic expansion. The Council entrusted him with the significant authority to establish lodges operating under the newly formulated

degrees and to appoint General Inspectors tasked with disseminating these practices to the New World.

Morin's endeavors would play a crucial role in the international spread of the Rite of Perfection, setting the stage for the global reach of the Ancient and Accepted Scottish Rite.

This period of Masonic history underscores the dynamic nature of the fraternity, reflecting its ability to adapt, evolve, and spread across borders, enriching its traditions with new layers of meaning and practice.

In America, the foundational structure of the High Degrees was further enriched with the addition of eight more degrees, culminating in the formation of *"The Ancient and Accepted Scottish Rite"* in 1801 in Charleston.

This expansion and formalization represented a significant evolution of the Rite, which then made a pivotal return to Paris in 1804, led by Count Alexander de Grasse-Tilly.

This marked a moment of full circle for the Rite, which had its early conceptual roots in the European Masonic traditions before being expanded and codified in the United States.

The dissemination and formalization of the Rite's practices took a significant leap forward by publishing the first printed ritual for the Entered Apprentice, Fellow Craft, and Master Mason degrees of the "*Ancient and Accepted Scottish Rite.*"

This publication, titled "*Guide de Masons Ecossais*" and released between 1825 and 1830, served as a foundational text for the Scottish Rite.

Its influence extended far beyond France, shaping the practices of Scottish-type rituals across continental Europe and various South American countries.

"Guide de Masons Ecossais" thus became a cornerstone for Masonic practice, encapsulating the essence and detailed rituals of the first three degrees of the Scottish Rite.

Its publication marked a crucial step in the

standardization and spread of the Rite, providing a comprehensive and authoritative source for Masons worldwide.

Through this guide, the Ancient and Accepted Scottish Rite established a lasting legacy, influencing the structure and execution of Masonic rituals in various cultural and national contexts.

The symbolic degrees within the Scottish-type rituals draw their foundational structure from the "Ancient" rituals of England, a lineage enriched and expanded by French Lodges towards the close of the 18th century and the dawn of the 19th.

In addition to the foundational rituals of the Ancients, these Lodges incorporated elements that reflected a broader, more esoteric spectrum of influences, including alchemy, hermeticism, and chivalry.

This synthesis of traditions resulted in a unique blend of Masonic practice that retained the core principles and symbols of the original English rituals and embraced a deeper, more mystical dimension.

The inclusion of alchemical symbols and hermetic teachings introduced an element of the transformational and philosophical into the Masonic journey, inviting members to engage in a more profound exploration of both the material and spiritual worlds.

On the other hand, the chivalric components emphasized virtues such as honor, loyalty, and bravery, echoing the knightly qualities that Freemasonry admires and aspires to instill in its members.

This enriched approach to the symbolic degrees marked a significant evolution in Freemasonry, reflecting a growing interest among Freemasons in the mysteries of the universe and the potential for personal transformation.

Integrating these diverse elements into the Scottish-type rituals underscored Freemasonry's adaptability and inclusiveness, demonstrating its capacity to absorb and reflect a wide array of cultural and philosophical influences while maintaining a cohesive and meaningful moral and spiritual development system.

THE RITUAL OF THE SYMBOLIC DEGREES OF THE FRENCH RITE

Speculative Freemasonry made its way to France around 1725, introduced by English emigrants who had

fled their homeland due to political upheaval following the overthrow of the Stuart dynasty.

These emigrants carried with them the practices and rituals of the brethren from the Grand Lodge of London, many of which bore the modifications instituted by the Grand Lodge post-1730, characteristic of the "Moderns" approach to Masonic ritual.

Upon their arrival in France, these rituals underwent further transformation. They were translated into French and enriched with elements unique to French

culture, weaving the local ethos and traditions into the fabric of Masonic practice. This cultural integration and adaptation process gave birth to what is known today as the "French Rite."

The cornerstone of the French Rite is the "Regulateur du Macon," published in 1801.

This seminal document serves as a comprehensive guide and authoritative source for the practices and principles of the French Rite. It encapsulates the refined synthesis of English Masonic practices and French cultural influences.

The *"Regulateur du Macon"* is a testament to Freemasonry's dynamic nature, highlighting its ability to cross cultural boundaries and incorporate diverse traditions into a unified system of moral and philosophical teachings.

Through this integration, the French Rite has established itself as a distinct and vital strand within the broader tapestry of global Freemasonry, contributing to the rich diversity of Masonic expression and practice.

THE INFLUENCE OF THE FRENCH LODGES OVER THE ORIGINAL RITUALS PUBLISHED IN ENGLAND

The French Lodges introduced various distinctive elements to the Masonic rituals that had originated in England before 1813.

France's cultural and philosophical milieu profoundly influenced these additions during the latter half of the 18th century and the early decades of the 19th century.

This period, marked by intellectual enlightenment

Paris Initiation circa 1750s

and revolutionary ideas, they have provided a fertile ground for integrating unique French characteristics into the traditional Masonic framework.

These modifications reflected the rich tapestry of French culture and thought, incorporating philosophical ideals, artistic sensibilities, and the values of liberty, equality, and fraternity that were emblematic of the era.

Through this process, the rituals practiced within French Lodges became a mirror of the societal

transformations occurring in France, embedding a distinctly French perspective on morality, ethics, and the pursuit of knowledge within Freemasonry.

This infusion of French cultural and philosophical elements into Masonic rituals underscored the fraternity's adaptability and capacity to embrace and reflect human experience and thought diversity.

The enriched rituals offered members a Masonic experience that was both universal in its principles and distinctly local in its expression, illustrating the dynamic interplay between global traditions and national identities within the fabric of Freemasonry.

Within the rituals of the French Rite and the Scottish Rite's symbolic degrees for Entered Apprentice, Fellow Craft, and Master Masons, several innovative elements were introduced, enriching the Masonic tradition with unique practices and symbols.

These additions, reflective of the cultural and philosophical depth of their times, include:

The Lodge's Trestle Board

A symbolic representation of the Master Mason's plans and designs, serving as a visual guide for the moral and ethical construction of one's life.

The Three Initiatic Journeys and the Four Trials

Symbolic voyages the candidate undertakes, representing the elemental trials of Earth, Air, Water, and Fire, each embodying a specific aspect of human experience and the purification process.

The Reflection Chamber

A preparatory space where candidates contemplate their upcoming initiation, symbolizing a period of introspection and mental preparation before embarking on their Masonic journey.

The Clapping and the Acclamation

Ritualistic expressions of unity and affirmation among brethren, the Clapping being a collective sound

made with hands or tools, and the Acclamation a vocal endorsement of the candidate's initiation.

The Usage of Swords for the Investment of the Candidates

A chivalric element that adds a layer of solemnity and tradition to the ceremony, symbolizing the candidate's readiness to defend their virtues and the principles of Freemasonry.

The Five Journeys of the Fellow Craft and Their Specific Elements

These further trials for the Fellow Craft degree extend the initiatic journeys and deepen the candidate's understanding and commitment to the Masonic path.

These elements, among others, signify Freemasonry's rich tapestry of symbolism and ritual, drawing from a diverse array of cultural and historical sources.

They serve not only as a means of conveying

Masonic teachings but also as a bridge connecting the fraternity's past with the present, allowing each generation of Freemasons to interpret and apply these timeless principles within their lives and societies.

Following their introduction, these innovative elements within the French and Scottish Rite symbolic degree rituals were adopted and adapted by various other Masonic rituals associated with the symbolic degrees.

Notably, such adaptations can be seen in the Schroeder ritual, the symbolic degree rituals of the Swedish Rite, the Rectified Scottish Rite, and other Masonic practices that emerged after the 19th century.

This cross-pollination of ritual elements across different Masonic traditions underscores Freemasonry's dynamic and interconnected nature.

As these modifications spread, they enriched the Masonic experience, allowing each Rite to imbue these elements with unique philosophical and cultural nuances.

Adopting these practices across various rites speaks to the universal appeal of their underlying themes, such as introspection, purification, unity, and pursuit of moral and ethical excellence, while highlighting the fraternity's diversity.

Incorporating these elements, each Rite contributed to a broader, more diverse Masonic tapestry, offering members multiple pathways to explore and embody Freemasonry's core values.

The spread of these ritual elements beyond their origins reflects the evolving nature of Masonic practice. It demonstrates how traditional forms can be adapted to meet the needs and sensibilities of different times and cultures, thus ensuring Freemasonry's continued relevance and vitality across the globe.

THE TWO DIRECTIONS OF THE MEANING OF THE MASONIC CEREMONY OF INITIATION

Within Freemasonry's broad and diverse spectrum, the initiation ceremonies can generally be categorized

along two distinct trajectories, reflective of the rich traditions and philosophical underpinnings of the Universal Masonic Chain.

These paths symbolize the cultural and historical contexts from which they emerge, offering unique perspectives on the symbolic journey of initiation into the fraternity.

Masonic Initiation Ceremonies, rich in symbolism and tradition, are predominantly shaped by two significant cultural streams: the Anglo-Saxon Rituals

and the combined traditions of French and Scottish Rituals.

Each stream offers a distinct approach and perspective on the initiation process, reflecting Freemasonry's diverse heritage and philosophical underpinnings.

The intersection of these two primary directions in Masonic Initiation Ceremonies highlights the fraternity's universal appeal and capacity to adapt to its members' cultural contexts.

Whether through the direct moral teachings of the Anglo-Saxon rituals or the symbolic and philosophical explorations of the French and Scottish traditions, Freemasonry invites its initiates to embark on a transformative journey of self-improvement, moral reflection, and spiritual enlightenment.

CEREMONY OF INITIATION IN ANGLO-SAXON RITUALS

This category encompasses the rituals practiced predominantly in English-speaking countries, such as those in the United Kingdom and the United States.

Anglo-Saxon rituals are characterized by their structured formality, emphasis on scriptural morality, and the symbolic use of the tools of operative masonry to impart ethical lessons.

These rituals reflect the pragmatic and moralistic ethos of the Anglo-Saxon cultural sphere, focusing on the personal development of the individual Mason through a series of progressive degrees.

Within the Anglo-Saxon Masonic tradition, the initiation ceremony holds a profound significance, primarily emphasizing the candidate's exercise of free will.

It is pivotal that the decision to join the Order comes from the individual's own volition, free from any external coercion or persuasion.

This principle underscores the Masonic cornerstone of individual liberty, affirming that true commitment to the fraternity's ideals starts with a personal and conscious choice.

Furthermore, the initiation process poignantly reminds the candidate of the value of discretion regarding Masonic teachings and symbols.

This ceremony aspect fosters a sense of mystery and exclusivity around the Order. It instills a deep respect for the sanctity of the fraternal bonds and shared knowledge within Freemasonry.

The emphasis on secrecy is integral to maintaining

the Order's unique identity and ensures that its traditions and wisdom are preserved with integrity for future generations.

The ceremonies are marked by clear and direct communication, focusing on the practical application of Masonic principles in daily life.

This approach resonates with the pragmatic and orderly spirit of the Anglo-Saxon tradition, emphasizing duty, responsibility, and brotherhood's social aspects.

CEREMONY OF INITIATION IN FRENCH AND SCOTTISH RITUALS

In contrast, the rituals practiced in France and those influenced by the Scottish Rite often incorporate a broader range of esoteric and philosophical elements, drawing from a wider spectrum of cultural and mystical traditions.

These ceremonies are distinguished by including themes from alchemy, hermeticism, and the chivalric tradition, weaving a rich tapestry of symbolic meaning that extends beyond the more straightforward moral instruction of the Anglo-Saxon rites.

French and Scottish rituals emphasize Mason's spiritual and intellectual enlightenment journey. They reflect the continental European affinity for abstract philosophical inquiry and the integration of diverse cultural influences, including liberty, equality, and fraternity. They are imbued with a spirit of questioning and intellectual exploration.

Scottish traditions, deeply influenced by the historical Knights Templar and Scotland's storied past, introduce elements of chivalry, loyalty, and the quest for spiritual insight.

Together, these traditions offer a more introspective and symbolic journey through the degrees of Freemasonry, encouraging initiates to seek deeper meanings and connections within the craft and beyond.

In a distinct departure from the Anglo-Saxon tradition, the initiation ceremonies found within French Masonry, as well as those akin to the

Scottish-type rituals prevalent among numerous Masonic Lodges integrate a rich layer of esoteric and

initiatory components.

Key among these are the Symbolic Journeys, the invocation of Fundamental Elements, and the contemplative experience of the Chamber of Reflection, among other profound additions.

These esoteric elements deepen the initiation process, framing it not merely as a formal entry into the fraternity but as the commencement of a profound inner quest.

This journey is aimed at the aspirant's spiritual

awakening and the pursuit of enlightenment.

Through these symbolic experiences, the candidate is invited to embark on a path of self-discovery and philosophical exploration, underscoring the transformative potential of Masonic initiation.

This approach highlights a holistic view of initiation, encompassing the external allegiance to Masonic values and the internal journey towards greater wisdom and understanding.

Within this rich tradition, Initiation transcends mere

formal acceptance into the Order, evolving into a quest for wisdom and a deeper comprehension of the self and the surrounding world.

The nuanced meaning of Initiation into Freemasonry is shaped by the distinct traditions and rituals specific to each Lodge, reflecting a diversity of approaches to the Masonic journey.

Despite these variations, Initiation consistently stands as a pivotal and profound milestone for the candidate, signifying the onset of a path marked by continuous learning, self-exploration, and spiritual growth within the framework of Freemasonry.

This initiation ceremony is not just an entrance rite but a symbolic gateway to a lifelong journey of enlightenment and fraternal bonds, underscoring the transformative essence of Masonic practice.

OFFICIALS OF THE LODGE IN THE ANGLO-SAXON RITUALS

Freemasonry's foundation is built upon ritualistic ceremonies, each demanding its members' active participation in crucial roles.

These roles are indispensable, contributing significantly to the ceremonial proceedings and the lodge's broader administrative and governance framework. The leadership team, which guides and oversees the lodge's functions and rituals, is central to this organized structure.

A specific set of officer positions exists in a Masonic Lodge that practices the Emulation Ritual, a ritual known for its precision and adherence to tradition. Each officer assumes a distinct and essential role within the lodge, ensuring the smooth operation and perpetuation of Freemasonry's esteemed ceremonies and values.

Each of these roles, while distinct, works in concert within the framework of the Emulation Ritual, embodying the principles of brotherly love, relief, and truth that Freemasonry espouses. Through their dedicated service, the officers of a Masonic Lodge contribute to their fraternity's enduring legacy and vibrant life.

Worshipful Master (WM)

Essentially, the principal officer of the lodge presides over meetings and ceremonies as the ceremonial head. He is responsible for upholding the lodge's bylaws, setting the tone for the lodge's work, and being the primary representative of the lodge in the wider Masonic community.

Senior Warden (SW)

As the second-in-command, he assists the Worshipful Master and steps in during their absence.

This role often involves overseeing the practical and moral welfare of the lodge members.

Junior Warden (JW)

The third principal officer oversees the lodge's harmony and works closely with the Senior Warden to assist the Worshipful Master.

He also plays a crucial role in social functions and is traditionally responsible for the festive board or lodge refreshments.

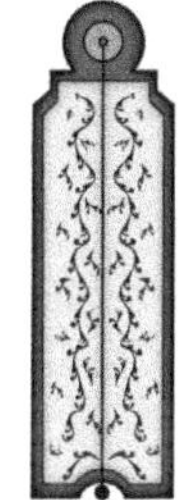

Treasurer

The treasurer manages the lodge's finances, including collecting dues, paying bills, and maintaining accurate financial records.

He ensures the lodge's economic stability and integrity.

Secretary

He acts as the administrative heart of the Lodge and is responsible for keeping minutes, correspondence, membership records, and official documents.

He is vital for the lodge's efficient operation and historical continuity.

Senior Deacon (SD)

Functions as the messenger for the Worshipful Master, facilitating communication within the lodge.

Has a ceremonial role that involves assisting the Worshipful Master and Senior Warden, guiding candidates during rituals.

Junior Deacon (JD)

Similar to the Senior Deacon, assisting the Junior Warden and helping guide candidates, as well as serving as a messenger and ensuring proper lodge protocol.

Senior Steward (SS) and Junior Steward (JS)

Both act as pages, often responsible for the logistical support of lodge activities and events, assisting in the preparation of the lodge room, and ensuring the comfort of members and visitors during ceremonies.

Marshall

It is responsible for the orderly conduct of rituals and processions.

Inner Guard

Stationed inside the lodge door, he ensures that only those duly qualified are allowed entry, assisting Tyler in securing the lodge meetings.

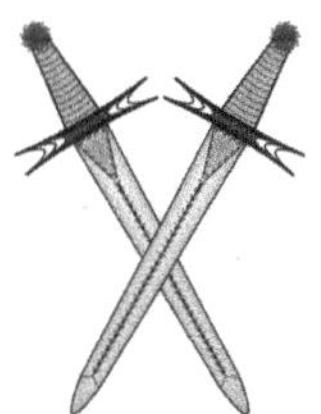

Tyler (or Tiler)

Positioned outside the lodge room, it guards against unauthorized entry and ensures that the lodge is free from disturbances during its work.

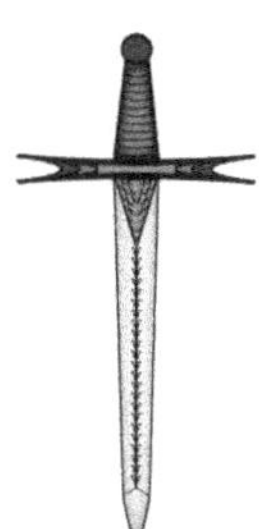

Chaplain

Provides spiritual support to the lodge, leading prayers and guidance in the moral and spiritual aspects of lodge ceremonies.

Each of these positions contributes to the seamless operation of the lodge, embodying the principles of Freemasonry and ensuring the integrity of its rituals and traditions.

OFFICIALS OF THE LODGE IN FRENCH AND SCOTTISH RITUALS

The rituals of French and Scottish origin are richly layered with historical and mystical elements, notably influenced by the storied legacy of the Knights Templar

and Scotland's profound historical narrative.

These traditions have modified the conventional roles and responsibilities of Lodge officers, imbuing the ceremonies with unique practices that reflect their deep historical roots and esoteric interests.

In these rituals, auditory cues significantly enhance the ceremonial atmosphere and mark critical moments. This is evidenced by multiple hammer strikes, the Master of Ceremonies punctuating specific ritual segments by striking the Temple floor with his staff or

creating a rhythmic clap reminiscent of a drum.

Such sound signals contribute to the ceremonies' solemnity and more military background, underscoring their significance and invoking a sense of continuity with ancient Templar traditions.

Certain lodge positions are elevated in importance within the context of French and Scottish Rites, reflecting these traditions' unique priorities and values.

Given that the Temples or meeting places of these Lodges were often secluded, secure, and remote,

ensuring privacy and uninterrupted conduct of rituals, the role of the outer guard or Tyler, traditionally tasked with securing the Lodge from external disturbances, became less critical in these contexts.

Additionally, the functions of the Chaplain, who provides spiritual guidance, and the Organist, who adds a musical dimension to the ceremonies while enriching, are not deemed essential in these traditions, allowing for flexibility in ritual practice.

The ten basic Lodge positions central to the French and Scottish Rites reflect a streamlined yet profound approach to Masonic governance and ceremony, tailored to the distinctive historical and esoteric influences shaping these rich Masonic traditions.

Worshipful Master (WM)

Acting as the guiding force and ceremonial head, he presides over Lodge activities and ceremonies, embodying the leadership and principles of Freemasonry in his stewardship.

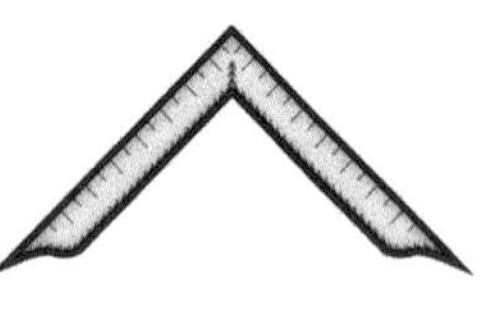

Senior Warden (SW)

Acts as the first vice president. He instructs and supervises Fellow Craft members of the Lodge, ensuring that members advance appropriately through the Masonic journey.

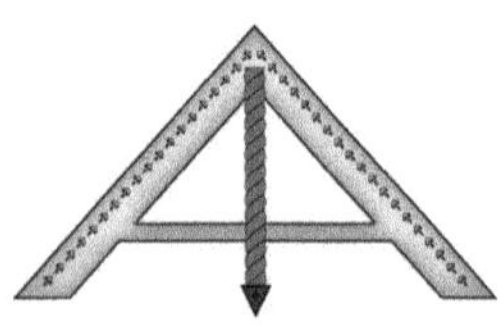

Junior Warden (JW)

As the second vice-president, he mirrors the responsibilities of the Senior Warden.

Still, he is specifically tasked with the guidance and supervision of Entered Apprentice Masons, fostering their initial steps within the fraternity.

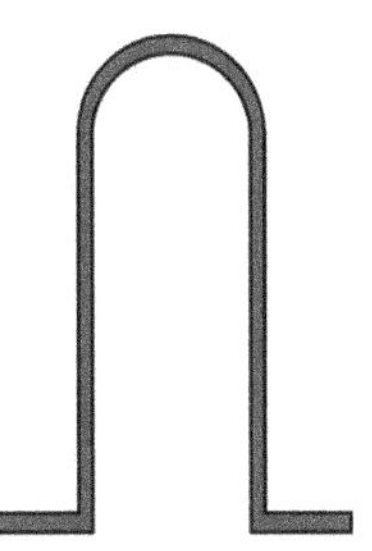

Orator

He maintains the Masonic legal framework, ensuring the Lodge's activities align with Masonic laws and traditions.

In some European jurisdictions (Germany, Austria, France, …), he also plays a critical role as a prosecutor in disciplinary proceedings, acting as a guardian of Masonic ethics and unity.

Secretary

He is the administrative anchor of the Lodge, responsible for documenting meetings, maintaining minutes, managing correspondence, and preserving the official records, thereby ensuring the continuity and organizational integrity of the Lodge.

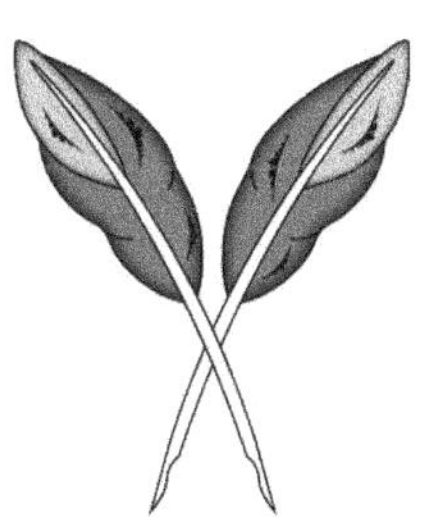

Treasurer

He oversees the lodge's financial health, managing funds, budgeting, and financial transactions, securing fiscal stability for charitable works and operational needs.

Expert

Tasked with the integrity of Masonic work, he prepares initiates for their entrance into the Lodge and introduces newcomers, ensuring that the sacred traditions and rituals are conveyed and understood with reverence.

Master of Ceremonies

Ensuring the seamless execution of Masonic Rituals and Ceremonies, he is responsible for the ceremonial aspects of Lodge meetings, from processions to the precise conduct of rituals.

Hospitaller

He manages the Lodge's charitable endeavors, from overseeing funds designated for philanthropy to supporting brethren in need, embodying Freemasonry's commitment to brotherly love and relief.

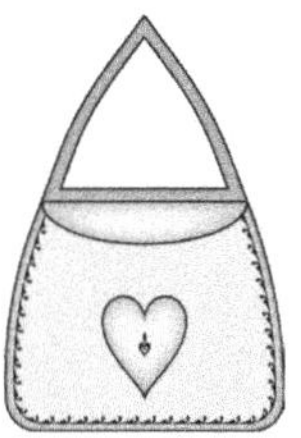

Tyler

Positioned at the inner door, he secures the sanctity of the Lodge meetings, ensuring that only duly qualified individuals participate, safeguarding the privacy and solemnity of the Masonic proceedings.

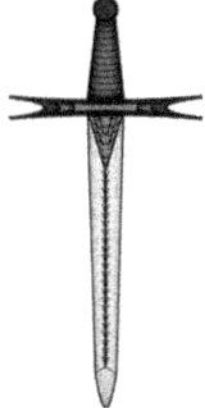

Together, these roles constitute the backbone of a Lodge within the French and Scottish Rites, each officer contributing to the rich tapestry of Masonic tradition and the lodge's effective operation.

These officers uphold Freemasonry's timeless values and principles through dedicated service, fostering growth, unity, and charity.

MASONIC RITUALS AND CEREMONIES

Generally speaking, in this modern period of universal Freemasonry, where freedom of movement is significant, we see several types of Masonic Rituals.

The Ritual is defined as a characteristic of Masonic activity. It is made to point out and explain the three symbolic degrees for which a Grand Lodge does not share its authority with anyone.

In addition to the Rituals of the 3 Degrees, some specific Rituals contain the opening and closing stages of the respective theme (Mourning, Consecration, etc).

First, we must understand that a Ritual is a sequence of activities involving gestures, words, actions, or objects performed according to a set sequence.

The immemorial traditions of Freemasonry prescribe rituals.

By definition, a Ritual is the unfolding of a flow that has a specific terminology, whereby from "nothing," from the "zero moments" in which you find yourself in a defined area, a succession of activities involving gestures, words, actions or objects begins, carried out based on an established sequence, until it comes to the point that within the space, among those present, a leap to another spiritual level is agreed upon, with a guarantee of the achievement of a specific framework equivalent to the conduct of activity in a Masonic Degree.

Each Grand Lodge, through its component Lodges, has approved different types of Masonic ceremonies in the armor of procedures and work activities in the Masonic Temple.

It is necessary to understand that a Ceremony is performed on a special occasion as part of a Ritual.

This is the significant difference between the two concepts.

Thus, within the Lodge, on the agenda of a Lodge opened and then closed by a Ritual approved by the Grand Lodge, different activities can be carried out without violating the mandatory principles to be respected regarding what can be discussed in the Temple within the Lodge.

These Ceremonies are accepted as long as they follow the basic rules of the Ritual and do not violate any provisions.

Freemasonry is publicly known through symbols, allegories, and principles. However, understanding what is public in a superficial theoretical way is useless if you do not know its exact meaning.

Thus, it is necessary to understand that each Grand Lodge, as an independent Jurisdiction, can adapt and personalize the Rituals of the three symbolic Degrees

with which it does not share its authority on the territory of the country it operates.

However, these Rituals personalization and adaptations have certain elements that can never be interfered with, as they are provided for in the ancient Landmarks and principles of recognition imposed by the United Grand Lodge of England.

RITUALS BASED ON LANDMARKS AND PRINCIPLES OF GRAND LODGE RECOGNITION

For those researching and interested in the various

types of Masonic Rituals existing and in progress throughout the world, it is essential to understand that certain common elements ensure the preservation of ancient Landmarks and the observance of the principles of regularity of recognition between the Grand Lodges and the United Grand Lodge of England.

In the specific case of the Rites of the Grand Lodges of the Universal Masonic Chain in the UGLE system of recognition, specific provisions refer to aspects of the Rites or the functioning of the Lodges (including the Ritual) that are obligatory to be respected and represent common points in all these types of rites, whatever their origin.

BASIC PRINCIPLES FOR GRAND LODGE RECOGNITION

Accepted by the Grand Lodge, September 4, 1929
Amended and adopted on 12 September 2018.

For ease of understanding, I will list these universally and unanimously accepted obligations, mark those that impact the Rituals, and represent common points to be respected.

1. *Regularity of origin;* i.e., each Grand Lodge shall have been established lawfully by a duly recognized Grand Lodge or by three or more regularly constituted Lodges.

2. *That a belief in the G.A.O.T.U. and His revealed will shall be an essential qualification for membership.*

3. *That all Initiates shall take their Obligation on or in full view of the open Volume of the Sacred Law, by which is meant the revelation from above which is binding on the conscience of the particular individual who is being initiated.*

4. *That the membership of the Grand Lodge and individual Lodges shall be composed exclusively of those who were made Masons as men* and that each Grand Lodge shall have no Masonic association of any kind with bodies which make women Masons.

5. *That the Grand Lodge shall have sovereign jurisdiction over the Lodges under its control; i.e. that it shall be a responsible, independent, self-governing organization, with sole and undisputed authority over the Craft or Symbolic Degrees (Entered Apprentice, Fellow Craft, and Master Mason) within*

its Jurisdiction; and shall not in any way be subject to, or divide such authority with, a Supreme Council or other Power claiming any control or supervision over those degrees.

6. *That the three Great Lights of Freemasonry (namely, the Volume of the Sacred Law, the Square, and the Compasses) shall always be exhibited when the Grand Lodge or its subordinate Lodges are at work, the chief of these being the Volume of the Sacred Law.*

7. *That the discussion of religion and politics within the Lodge shall be strictly prohibited.*

8. *That the principles of the Ancient Landmarks, customs, and usages of the Craft shall be strictly observed.*

BASIC PRINCIPLES FOR GRAND LODGE RECOGNITION

In today's exploration of Masonic history, we delve into the venerable Ancient Landmarks of Freemasonry.

These Landmarks stand as immutable milestones,

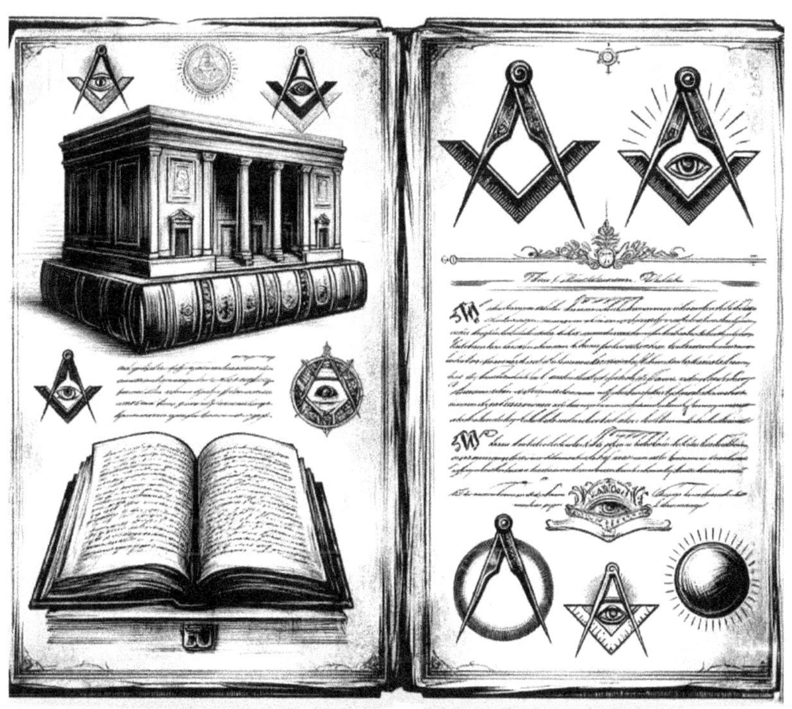

guiding the essence and defining the boundaries of Freemasonry itself. They serve as the foundational principles that delineate the scope of a Lodge, including Grand Lodges and Grand Orients, establishing the core upon which Freemasonry is built.

As outlined in the General Regulations by the Premier Grand Lodge of England in 1723 and further encapsulated in Anderson's Constitutions, it is stated: "*Every Annual Grand Lodge possesses the inherent authority to enact new regulations or modify existing ones for the genuine advancement of this age-old*

Brotherhood; on the condition that the ancient Landmarks are meticulously safeguarded."

This directive underscores the flexibility within the structure of Freemasonry to evolve, provided its timeless landmarks remain untouched.

Despite their critical importance, these landmarks were never explicitly defined, leaving their exact nature shrouded in mystery and interpretation.

Initial exploration of the Ancient Landmarks of Freemasonry is engaging and provides a solid foundation for understanding their significance within the Masonic tradition. The narrative emphasizes the Landmarks' role as unchangeable principles and defining elements of Freemasonry's identity.

Moreover, your reference to historical documents adds an authoritative depth to your discussion, grounding it in the rich history of Freemasonry.

To enhance your writing further, consider weaving in examples or hypothetical scenarios that illustrate the practical application or impact of these landmarks on the practices and governance of Freemasonry. Doing so could offer readers a more tangible understanding of their importance and how they have shaped the fraternity over centuries. Additionally, exploring the ambiguity surrounding the Landmarks' definitions and how this has influenced Masonic tradition and interpretation over time could add an intriguing layer of complexity to your narrative.

In the mid-19th century, the conversation about the precise nature of Masonic Landmarks took a more defined shape through the contributions of notable Masonic scholars.

In 1844, George Oliver noted the diversity in understanding Masonic landmarks across different jurisdictions. He said that some jurisdictions strictly limited the definition of a Masonic landmark to *"signs, tokens, and words."*

In contrast, others expanded it to include the ceremonial processes of initiation, passing, and raising a candidate within the fraternity.

A dozen years later, in 1856, Albert Mackey further enriched the discourse by enumerating what he considered to be the 25 ancient Landmarks of Freemasonry. Mackey didn't stop at just listing these landmarks; he ventured to delineate specific characteristics that, in his view, each landmark inherently possesses. These characteristics include a notional immemorial antiquity, suggesting that landmarks are rooted in the most profound history of Freemasonry; universality, indicating that these landmarks are recognized and upheld across the various Masonic jurisdictions worldwide; and an absolute "irrevocability," asserting that these landmarks are permanent and unalterable fixtures of Masonic tradition.

Mackey's framework suggests that while Grand Lodges can acknowledge any landmarks they see fit, the landmarks they choose to recognize significantly influence their fraternal relationships.

Specifically, the landmarks a Grand Lodge recognizes can impact whether it is acknowledged by other Grand Lodges, highlighting the interconnectedness of Masonic jurisdictions through shared or divergent understandings of these foundational principles.

The text provides an insightful overview of the historical perspectives on Masonic landmarks, particularly highlighting the contributions of George Oliver and Albert Mackey to the discourse. By focusing on their interpretations, you effectively illustrate the evolving understanding of what constitutes a Masonic landmark.

To enrich the exploration further, it might be considered to delve into the implications of Mackey's criteria for a landmark's recognition and how this has influenced Masonic practices and inter-jurisdictional relations.

Additionally, examining the debates or controversies arising from the varying interpretations of landmarks could offer readers a deeper understanding of the complexities and nuances within Masonic tradition.

This approach would provide historical context and illuminate the ongoing evolution of Masonic identity and governance.

"The first great duty, not only of every Lodge but of every Mason, is to see that the landmarks of the Order shall never be impaired." **Albert Mackey (1856)**

For ease of understanding, I will list these 25 landmarks of Freemasonry as defined in 1856 by Albert

Mackey (1807-1881) as universally and unanimously accepted obligations.

I will mark those that impact the rituals and represent common points that must be respected.

1. The fraternal modes of recognition
2. The division of Masonry into three symbolic degrees
3. The symbolic legend of Hiram Abiff
4. The government of the fraternity by a Grand Master
5. The prerogative of the Grand Master to preside

over every assembly of the craft

6. The prerogative of the Grand Master to issue dispensations for conferring degrees at irregular times

7. The prerogative of the Grand Master to issue dispensations for opening and holding Lodges otherwise not established

8. The prerogative of the Grand Master to make Masons at Sight

9. The necessity for Masons to congregate in Lodges

10. The government of Lodges to be by a Master and two Wardens

11. The necessity that every Lodge, when congregated, be duly tiled

12. The right of every Mason to be represented in all general meetings of the Craft

13. The right of every Mason to appeal from his Lodge's decisions to the Grand Lodge

14. The right of every Mason to sit in every regular Lodge

15. That no unknown visitor be allowed to sit in the Lodge without being examined and found to be a Freemason

16. That no Lodge can interfere in the business of another Lodge

17. That every Freemason be amenable to the laws

and regulations of the Jurisdiction in which he resides

18. That candidates for Freemasonry be required to meet specific qualifications, namely: being a man of mature age, not a cripple, and free-born

19. That a belief in the existence of God be a requirement for membership

20. That belief in a resurrection to a future life be a requirement for membership

21. That a "Book of the Law" shall constitute an indispensable part of the furniture of every Lodge

22. The equality of Masons

23. The secrecy of the Institution

24. The foundation of a speculative science upon an operative art and the symbolic use and explanation of the terms of that art for purposes of moral teaching

25. That none of these landmarks can be changed.

In 1911, understanding Mackey's 25 points to be a summary of Masonic *"common law,"* the legal scholar Roscoe Pound (1870–1964) distinguished seven of them as landmarks:

1. Belief in a Supreme Being (19)
2. Belief in immortality (20)
3. That a "book of sacred law" is an indispensable part of the "furniture" (or furnishings) of the Lodge (21)
4. The legend of the Third Degree (3)
5. Secrecy (not specified as to what) (11, 23)
6. Symbolism of operative masonry (24)
7. That a Mason must be a man, freeborn, and of lawful age (18)

CONCLUSION

In summary, Freemasonry's harmonious blend of uniformity and diversity is vividly reflected through

the distinctive variations and, intriguingly, in the unique character of the various rites.

Certain firmly established foundational elements must remain unaltered, uncustomed, unreplaced, and intact to maintain consistency and safeguard Freemasonry's heritage.

These unchangeable components serve as the bedrock upon which the rich tapestry of Freemasonry is woven.

Beyond these immutable core principles lies an

enriching path of exploration for those drawn to the mystique of Freemasonry.

This journey unveils the rich tapestry of differences, parallels, and singular aspects that adorn the ancient Rituals of Freemasonry. It's a testament to the fraternity's ability to hold fast to its venerable traditions while embracing the diverse expressions of its universal principles.

Your conclusion beautifully encapsulates the essence of Freemasonry as a blend of enduring traditions and diverse practices. Highlighting the importance of unchangeable elements in preserving Masonic heritage while also inviting exploration of the unique features of various Masonic Rituals offers a balanced view of the fraternity's complexity and appeal.

To further enrich your conclusion, consider providing a brief example or anecdote illustrating Freemasonry's dynamic interplay between tradition and diversity.

This could help to ground your abstract observations in real terms, making the enduring allure of Freemasonry's rituals and principles more tangible to the reader.